The Paralyzed Man

AMERICAN BIBLE SOCIETY
NEW YORK

The Paralyzed Man (Vol. 2)
Scripture quotes from the *Contemporary English Version,* Mark 2.1-12 (CEV).
Wording and grammar represent the kind of language best understood
and appreciated by young readers.

Copyright © 1995, American Bible Society
1865 Broadway, New York, N. Y. 10023
www.americanbible.org

Illustrations by Chantal Muller van den Berghe
Text by Bernard Hubler and Claude-Bernard Costecalde, Ph. D.
Design by Jacques Rey

Copyright © 1997, Éditions du Signe
Strasbourg, France

ISBN 1-58516-142-X
Printed in Italy
Eng. Port. CEV 560 P - 109859
ABS - 7/00 - 5,000

J
232.955
HUB

4

A person's body can be paralyzed from birth
or by a serious accident.
But people can be paralyzed in other ways—
by fear, by shyness, or by boredom.
Fear can paralyze us.
Noise or people who seem stronger can frighten us.
We can be afraid of being alone, of having no friends.
Shyness can paralyze us by making us unable
to look people in the eye.
Boredom can paralyze us and make days
and nights seem to last forever.
If these things ever paralyze you,
Then listen to what Jesus has to tell us.

Jesus went back to Capernaum.

Jesus often went back to Capernaum,
a small city located on the shores
of Lake Tiberius.
He felt at home there and every time
that he returned, crowds would gather
to hear him speak.
On this day the house was overflowing.

*When we see a crowd, we know
that something is happening.*

Four people came up, carrying a paralyzed man on a mat.

Jesus was teaching and the people knew
that it was not just all talk,
but that he did what he said.
He cured the sick.
Some people came to him, carrying a paralyzed man on a mat.

We can do very little by ourself.
We need others to help us
along the way.

But because of the crowd they could not get him to Jesus.

The big crowd prevented them
from getting close to Jesus.
No problem!
They had expected this
and knew exactly what to do.
They went out and looked for some strong rope.

To reach our goal we must first find the way.

So they made a hole in the roof above him...

Too bad for the roof.
They made a hole in it to lower
the mat on which the man lay.
A hole in the roof was a small price
to pay to have the paralyzed man healed.
They would be able to repair it later on.

*Sometimes we must
destroy in order to rebuild.*

... and let the man down in front of everyone.

Jesus was impressed.
He appreciated the boldness of these people.
It was proof of how much they trusted him.
He also saw a chance to put into practice
what he had been teaching the crowd.

*The person who takes no risks
will do nothing worthwhile.*

When Jesus saw how much faith they had, he said to the paralyzed man, "My friend, your sins are forgiven."

What was important for Jesus was to free this man from an even deeper pain: sin!

So he said to the paralyzed man, "Your sins are forgiven."

Behind the pain we can see, there is often suffering we can't see.

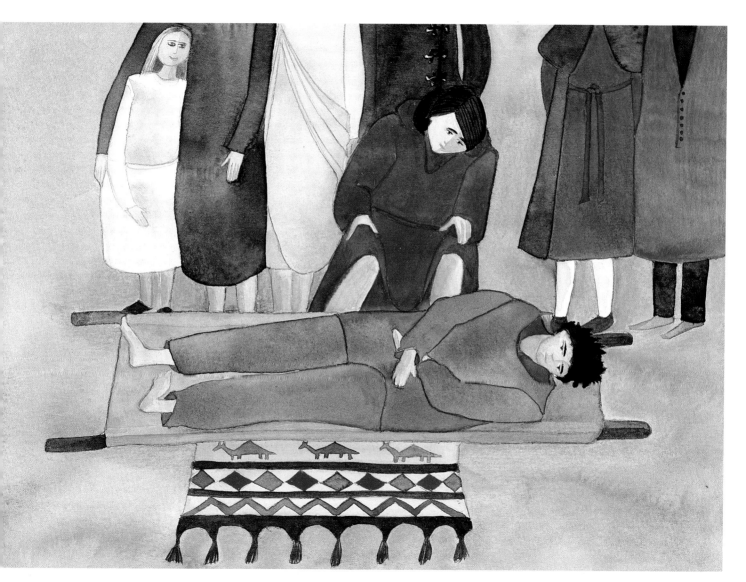

Some of the teachers of the Law… started wondering, "Why would he say such a thing? He must think he is God!"

"How does he dare talk like this?"
the teachers of the Law complained,
"Only God can forgive sins."
So Jesus used this occasion to show
that he is the Son of God
and that he has the power
to forgive sins.

People don't always recognize who we really are.

Jesus said to the paralyzed man, "Get up! Pick up your mat and go on home."

Jesus admired the faith
of those who carried
the paralyzed man to him.
He decided to cure the man.
He extended his hand and said:
"Get up! Pick up your mat
and go on home."

The person who believes in nothing won't go very far.

The man got right up.

The man got right up.
He was amazed
that he could move his legs.
He started to walk.
Everyone was amazed.
Jesus was glad.

It is wonderful to see life come back to someone who was lifeless.

Everyone watched in amazement.

The paralyzed man did not try
to understand what had just happened.
He did as he was told:
he picked up his mat and went home.
Everyone watched in amazement.
"We have never seen anything like this!"
And they all praised God.

If someone wants only the best for you,
do what the person tells you to do.

*As you can see,
this story can teach you many things.
For example, if you have a problem,
it is not necessarily your fault.
Speak to other people
about your problem;
maybe they can help you to solve it.
Never say,
"It's impossible, I'll never get better."
Believing that it is possible
gives you the strength you need to live happily.
This is what Jesus wants for you!*

Jesus went back to Capernaum.

Four people came up, carrying a paralyzed man on a mat.

So they made a hole in the roof above him...

But because of the crowd
they could not get him to Jesus.

When Jesus saw how much faith they had, he said to the paralyzed man, "My friend, your sins are forgiven."

Some of the teachers of the Law… started wondering, "Why would he say such a thing? He must think he is God!"

Jesus said to the paralyzed man, "Get up! Pick up your mat and go on home!"

Everyone watched in amazement.

… and let the man down in front of everyone.

The man got right up.

29

IN THE SAME COLLECTIONS:

The Good Samaritan
Zacchaeus
On the Road to Emmaus
Bartimaeus
The Call of the Disciples
The Calming of the Storm
Shared Bread
The Prodigal Son
An Amazing Catch
The Forgiven Sinner
The Farmer Who Went Out To Sow